NATURE'S MONSTERS

LIZARDS

Brenda Ralph Lewis

GARETH**STEVENS**
PUBLISHING
A Member of the WRC Media Family of Companies

This North American edition first published in 2006 by
Gareth Stevens Publishing
A Member of the WRC Media Family of Companies
330 West Olive Street, Suite 100
Milwaukee, WI 53212 USA

ISBN 13: 978-0-8368-6363-5
ISBN 10: 0-8368-6363-1

Original edition and illustrations copyright © 2006 by International Masters Publishers AB.
Produced by Amber Books Ltd., Bradley's Close, 74–77 White Lion Street, London N1 9PF, U.K.

Project editor: Michael Spilling
Design: Joe Conneally

Gareth Stevens editorial direction: Valerie J. Weber
Gareth Stevens art direction and cover design: Tammy West
Gareth Stevens production: Jessica Morris

Printed in China

1 2 3 4 5 6 7 8 9 10 09 08 07 06

Contents

Continents of the World

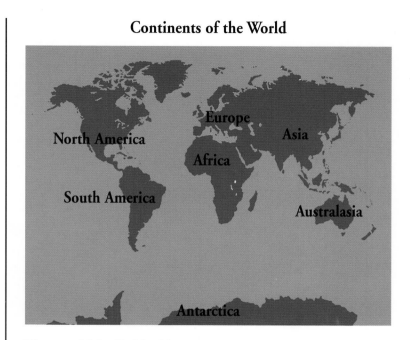

The world is divided into seven continents —
North America, South America, Europe, Africa,
Asia, Australasia, and Antarctica. In this book,
the area where each animal lives is shown in red,
while all land is shown in green.

Words that appear in the glossary are printed in
boldface type the first time they occur in the text.

Basilisk Lizard

The basilisk (BA-suh-lisk) **lizard**'s brown or green skin helps **camouflage** its body in bushes and other plants.

A basilisk lizard's long, thin tail keeps it upright when it is running.

The lizard can run at high speeds because of its strong, powerful legs.

Long fingers and sharp claws give the basilisk lizard a strong grip for climbing trees.

Basilisk lizards are also called "Jesus Christ" lizards. The Bible tells of Christ walking on water. Basilisk lizards can do that, too, because of the shape of their back feet.

Size

Did You Know?

There is a difference between the male and the female basilisk lizard. Only the male has a **crest** of skin that runs all the way from its head to its tail.

1 The lizard pushes each **webbed** foot down hard on the surface of the water to create pockets of air.

3 As the lizard runs along, its feet slowly sink into the water. It can run up to 65 feet (20 meters) before it sinks completely. Then it must start swimming instead.

2 When the lizard "runs" across the water, it is really running on these pockets of air.

Where in the World

Basilisk lizards live near rivers and streams in the thick forests of Central America and northern South America. They grow from 24 to 30 inches (61 to 76 centimeters) in length.

Ground Chameleon Lizard

Its dull, spiny skin camouflages the ground chameleon (kuh-MEEL-yun). It looks like dead leaves or tree bark.

The ground chameleon is a **ground dweller** and does not have a long, strong tail like a **tree-dwelling** lizard.

The chameleon's long sticky tongue shoots out quickly to snatch its **prey**.

The ground chameleon is tiny, no more than 4 inches (10 cm) long.

Male chameleons will often fight over food and **territory**. When two **rival** male chameleons fight, the battle can be fierce and deadly.

1 Each of these chameleons wants to drive his rival away. They start by staring each other in the eye, opening their mouths wide, and making angry side-to-side movements.

2 Neither chameleon is willing to move away, so they must fight. They fling themselves at each other, biting with their strong jaws and gripping with their thin but strong legs. The battle lasts until one of the lizards is too badly injured to continue.

Actual Size

Where in the World

There are about twenty-four species of ground chameleons. Most live on the island of Madagascar off the eastern coast of Africa. Others live in the **savannas** and **tropical** forests of Central Africa.

Jackson's Chameleon

Both male and female Jackson's chameleons have three horns on their heads.

The chameleon's tongue is 12 inches (30 cm) long — almost as long as the chameleon itself.

When hunting, the chameleon's eyes move forward to **focus** on its prey.

Nose to tail, Jackson's chameleon measures up to 12.5 inches (32 cm) long.

The Jackson's chameleon can judge the exact distance it must cover to grab the insects it eats as food. Then, it uses its long, muscled tongue to attack.

1 When it is not using it for hunting, the Jackson's chameleon's long tongue lies wrinkled up in its mouth.

2 When the chameleon is close enough to its prey, the sticky pad at the end of its tongue starts to hang out of its mouth. Moments later, the chameleon shoots out its tongue with great speed.

3 In only one-fourth of a second, the Jackson's chameleon has caught the prey with the end of its tongue and pulled it back into its mouth.

Size

Where in the World

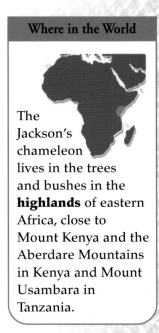

The Jackson's chameleon lives in the trees and bushes in the **highlands** of eastern Africa, close to Mount Kenya and the Aberdare Mountains in Kenya and Mount Usambara in Tanzania.

9

Panther Chameleon

The **chromatophores** in its skin enable the chameleon to change color.

The panther chameleon opens its mouth wide to eat insects and frighten rivals.

The panther chameleon can hang from tree branches using its strong, **flexible** tail.

Its curved toes allow the chameleon to grip the branches of trees very firmly.

The panther chameleon can be a fierce fighter. It has one unusual weapon — when it becomes really angry, it can change its colors as a warning to rivals and enemies.

On Madagascar, many people fear panther chameleons because of their fierce, colorful appearance. Cars and other traffic stop when a pantheon chameleon crosses the road.

1 A panther chameleon walking along a small branch comes face to face with a rival. The panther chameleon is determined to get rid of its smaller rival. As it grows more and more pushy, the chromatophores in its skin make its colors much brighter.

2 The colors of the larger panther chameleon change from dull green to dangerous-looking red and orange. The skin color of its much smaller rival gets paler and paler. At last, the rival decides to leave; it crawls away, defeated.

Where in the World

Most panther chameleons **inhabit rain forests** on the island of Madagascar off the eastern coast of Africa. They can also be found on other islands in the Indian Ocean, such as Nosi Bé, Réunion, and Mauritius.

11

Frilled
Lizard

The frill surrounds the frilled lizard's head except at the back of its neck.

With its mouth open, the lizard looks frightening, but it does not harm humans.

The frilled lizard has scales all over its body, like protective armor.

Wherever the frilled lizard lives, its skin color blends in with its surroundings.

Frilled lizards try to **bluff** their enemies away. These tricks, however, do not always work, so sometimes the lizard has to try something else.

Size

1 The frilled lizard is in danger. The first thing it does is keep still, hoping that its color will hide it from its enemy.

3 The lizard's enemy is not frightened away, so the lizard stands up on its back legs and waves its claws, jaws, and tail. If its enemy still is not frightened, the frilled lizard will give up and run away.

2 This trick does not work, so the lizard becomes threatening. It opens its mouth wide and uses two rods made of bone to spread out its big frill. It also hisses loudly.

Did You Know?

Together with the kangaroo, the frilled lizard is one of the symbols of Australia. This dramatic-looking **reptile** has appeared on the Australian two-cent coin and on the country's postage stamps.

Where in the World

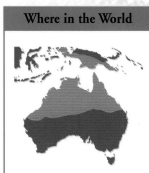

The frilled lizard lives in the tropical regions of northern Australia and southern Papua New Guinea.

Flying Lizard

It uses its long tail to help it change direction while gliding.

The flying lizard **glides** by spreading out flaps of skinlike wings.

The lizard's spotted skin allows it to hide when lying on tree trunks.

The flying lizard uses its strong feet to climb trees in its rain forest **habitats**.

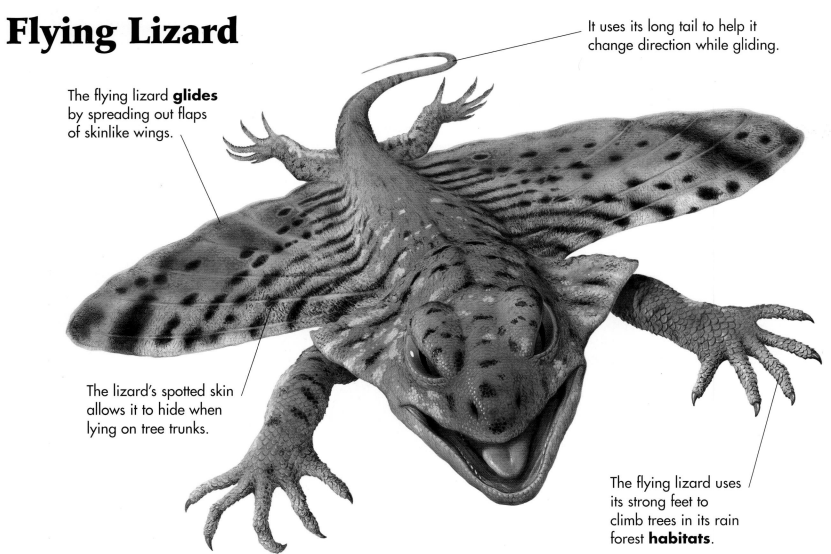

Flying lizards like to eat ants, termites, and other small insects, which they find on the trunks and branches of trees. They often surprise their prey with their ability to glide through the air.

1 The lizard sees a small beetle in a crack in the bark of a tree. Using its long tongue, it captures the beetle and eats it.

Size

Several other animals can also glide through the forest using flaps of skin. They include other lizards called geckos, squirrels, frogs, **marsupials**, and even a snake — the paradise tree snake.

2 It is still hungry, so the lizard moves on to another tree nearby. It spreads its bright yellow "wings" and jumps into the air.

3 The lizard flattens its body and steers with its tail to land on the tree trunk. It starts climbing up, looking for more food.

Where in the World

Flying lizards live in the rain forests of Southeast Asia, including the Philippines, Malaysia, and Indonesia. They share these habitats with forty similar species of lizard.

Gila Monster

The gila monster delivers its **venom** through its lower teeth. The teeth each have two **grooves**.

The gila (HE-luh) monster has scales like beads that help it to blend into the desert landscape.

The gila monster stores fat from food in its tail to support it through the winter.

This lizard has short, powerful legs with big claws on its feet.

Gila monsters are the only poisonous lizards in North America. They use their teeth or their venom to **paralyze** or kill their prey. Gila monsters swallow their prey in one piece.

Size

Did You Know?

The gila monster goes hunting for food only in the spring and summer. When it has eaten enough, it spends the winter lying around in a sandy **burrow**.

1 This gila monster has followed a small snake by using its **forked tongue** to "taste" its scent in the air. When it reaches its prey, the gila opens its mouth wide.

Where in the World

Gila monsters are North American lizards. In the United States, they can be found in New Mexico, California, Nevada, Arizona, and Utah and also in the state of Sonora in northwestern Mexico.

2 The lizard pounces. It seizes the snake by the neck, sinks its teeth into its flesh, and pumps in its venom through its grooved lower teeth.

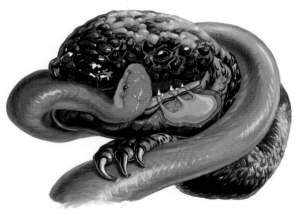

3 The little snake has no chance. Nothing can stop the gila monster from gulping it down head first. The snake vanishes inside the lizard.

Green Iguana

The reptile uses a flap of skin, or dewlap, under its throat to signal to other iguanas.

A mass of tiny scales covers the green iguana's (ih-GWAH-nuh) skin.

Green iguanas use scent **glands** under their thighs to mark their territory.

The iguana uses its long, sharp claws for climbing trees and digging.

Some people keep green iguanas as household pets, but they are not really tame like dogs, cats, or hamsters. Sometimes they still act like creatures living in the wild.

Size

1 A pet male green iguana sits on a bookshelf in a room where his owner is watching television. For the iguana, this room is his territory, and his owner looks like a rival.

Did You Know?

Green iguanas are often used to play dinosaurs in movies. In real life, they measure between 3 and 6 feet (0.9–1.8 meters), including the tail. Movie cameras make them look huge.

Where in the World

Green iguanas live in central Mexico, Central America, and the northern part of South America. They also live on some Caribbean islands, such as Trinidad and Tobago.

2 The green iguana moves his head up and down as a warning, but the owner does not notice.

3 The iguana becomes angry and attacks his owner, who tries to protect himself. The iguana gives him several painful bites and scratches.

Regal Horned Lizard

The horned lizard's large stomach can **digest** huge quantities of insects, such as harvester ants.

The lizard has spikes all over its body, even on its belly, for protection.

The round, flattened body of the regal horned lizard is unusually wide.

Regal horned lizards are often preyed upon by larger animals. Although their spiky appearance may put off some animals, their main defence is to squirt an irritating fluid at a predator.

1 The regal horned lizard turns to face an approaching skunk. The lizard stays very stiff and still. It closes its eyes — but not out of fear. It is preparing a nasty surprise for the skunk.

2 The skunk is fooled into thinking that the lizard is not going to defend itself. Suddenly, from underneath its closed eyelids, the lizard shoots out jets of blood straight into the skunk's face. Shocked and startled, the skunk runs away.

Did You Know?

This lizard can eat twenty–five hundred harvester ants in one meal. It is a slow eater and spends a long time in the intense heat of the desert while having its meals.

Where in the World

The regal horned lizard lives in the harsh, rocky Sonoran desert that covers northwestern Mexico and the U.S. states of Arizona and New Mexico.

Leaf-Tailed Gecko

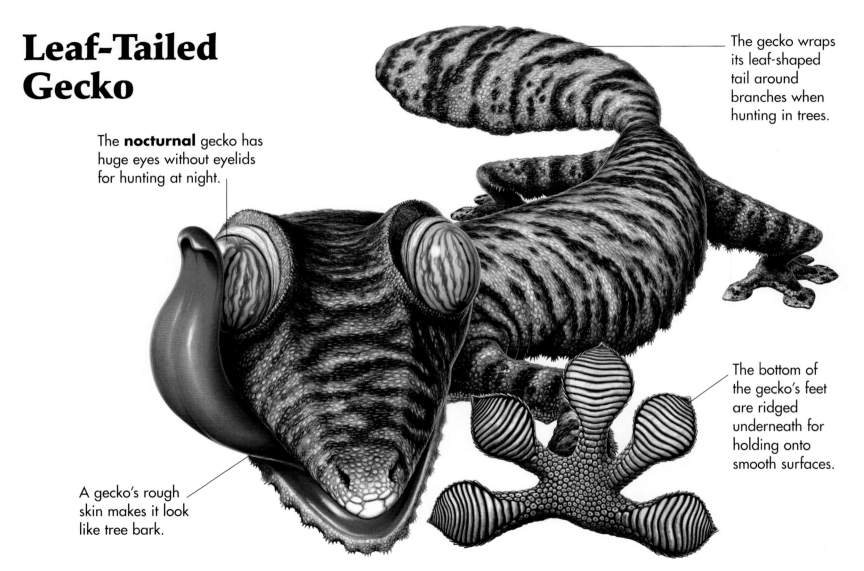

The gecko wraps its leaf-shaped tail around branches when hunting in trees.

The **nocturnal** gecko has huge eyes without eyelids for hunting at night.

A gecko's rough skin makes it look like tree bark.

The bottom of the gecko's feet are ridged underneath for holding onto smooth surfaces.

Small animals often hunt leaf-tailed geckos. Sometimes, the geckos will turn on their predators and hiss, hoping to frighten them away. At other times, they have to escape quickly to avoid being eaten.

1 The leaf-tailed gecko is suddenly disturbed by a wild cat that has climbed up the tree to eat the lizard. The gecko runs along the branch, and reaches the end.

Size

2 The gecko jumps off the branch into the air. As it plunges downward, the gecko rolls itself up into a tight ball. It hits the ground, bounces twice but is not hurt.

3 Out of danger, the gecko unravels and heads for the nearest dense bushes and grass to hide from any other predators.

Did You Know?

Because leaf-tailed geckos are active only after sunset, they cannot use the sun's heat to warm up. During the day, they sleep under tree bark to keep warm.

Where in the World

While other geckos live in every part of the world, leaf-tailed geckos can only be found on the island of Madagascar off the eastern coast of Africa.

Nile Monitor

The Nile monitor's brownish green and yellow skin color matches the riverside plant life.

The Nile monitor's thick, strong claws are used for climbing and for killing prey.

The Nile monitor defends itself against its enemies by flicking its long, powerful tail.

To warm its body, the Nile monitor lies on rocks in the morning sun.

The Nile monitor will eat small animals, such as snails, crabs, snakes, frogs, and small lizards, and the eggs of other reptiles and birds.

Size

1 A mother crocodile buries her eggs for safety in the warm sand by a river. A **mongoose** starts sniffing around the eggs. The crocodile roars loudly and drives the mongoose away.

2 While the crocodile is busy scaring the mongoose, she does not notice the Nile monitor creeping toward the buried eggs. Before she can stop the monitor, it quickly digs down into the sand, then snatches an egg and runs off into a bush to eat it.

Where in the World

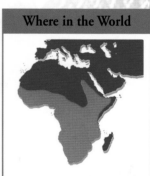

Although Nile monitors are named after the Nile River in Egypt, they do not only live there. They also live near rivers in every part of Africa.

Salvadori's Monitor

The Salvadori's monitor's (SAL-vuh-DOOR-ees MAH-nuh-tur) tail is twice as long as its body and is used as a whip.

The Salvadori's monitor has extralong toes and sharp, curved claws for climbing trees.

It has teeth as sharp as razors and inflicts terrible bites.

As a male Salvadori's monitor ages, its **snout** becomes much wider.

Salvadori's monitor lizards have poor eyesight and sometimes panic when surprised away from their treetop habitat.

1 A tourist on vacation in New Guinea sees a Salvadori's monitor and decides to take a photograph.

2 As the tourist moves closer, the lizard becomes scared. It tries to run up the nearest tree to get away, but the tourist is the first upright shape it sees. Mistaking him for a tree, the monitor runs up the tourist instead! They are both very scared as they come face to face.

Size

Did You Know?

Salvadori's monitors spend most of their lives high up in the trees in the New Guinea rain forests. The first one was not discovered until 1878.

Where in the World

Salvadori's monitor lizards live in a very small area — in the tropical forests and **mangrove** swamps in southern New Guinea, an island in Southeast Asia.

27

Bearded Dragon

Extralarge scales around the lizard's eyes protect them from dirt and sand.

An adult male bearded dragon has a dark "beard," which turns black when he is trying to attract a mate.

When predators threaten, the lizard escapes fast on its short, strong legs.

The bearded dragon has a pouch on its throat that is covered in spines.

In the morning, some bearded dragon lizards **absorb** heat by **basking** in the sun. Although they can look threatening, they are not dangerous to people.

1 The sun has just risen in the sky. A bearded dragon lizard climbs a fence to warm itself in the sun's rays. A little girl sees the lizard leaning on the fence post.

2 She runs across the grass to have a closer look at it. The bearded dragon lizard thinks she is going to attack. It puffs up its body and spreads its spines to make itself look larger than it really is. The little girl runs away in fright.

Size

Where in the World

There are seven species of bearded dragon lizard living in Australia in dry deserts, grasslands, forests, **scrubland** and wet coastal areas. Only five of the seven species have "beards."

Glossary

absorb — to take something in

basking — lying down in the sun to gain warmth

bluff — to trick or frighten by pretending to have some power or strength

burrow — an underground home dug by an animal

camouflage — to disguise or hide

chromatophores — skin cells that can change color in many lizards and some other animals

crest — a raised line or ridge of skin on an animal

digest — to break down food in the body

flexible — able to bend easily without breaking

focus — to look at very closely

forked tongue — a tongue split into two parts at the end

glands — parts of the body that make special chemicals needed for the body to work properly

glides — to move through the air without flying

grooves — hollow channels or marks

ground dweller — an animal that lives on the ground

habitats — places where an animal usually lives

highlands — lands high up in the mountains or hills

inhabit — to live in

lizard — one of a large group of reptiles that have long, scaly bodies, four legs, and a pointed tail

mangrove — any evergreen tree or shrub with stiltlike roots that grows thickly along coasts

marsupials — animals that carry their young in pouches, including kangaroos, opossums, and wombats

mongoose — a cat-sized mammal that eats fruit and small animals

nocturnal — active at night

paralyze — to make it impossible to move

predators — animals that hunt other animals for food

prey — an animal hunted for food

reptile — air-breathing creature that usually has a body covered with scaly or bony plates, including alligators, lizards, and snakes

rain forests — thick forests where a lot of rain falls

rival — competing over the same thing

savannas — open grasslands, scattered with bushes and trees

scrublands — lands covered with small shrubs or trees

snout — short, flat nose

territory — land that an animal claims as its own

tree-dwelling — living in trees

tropical — referring to the warmest regions of the world, with lush plant life and lots of rain

venom — a poison made by an animal

webbed — covered in a thin layer of skin

Contents

Continents of the World

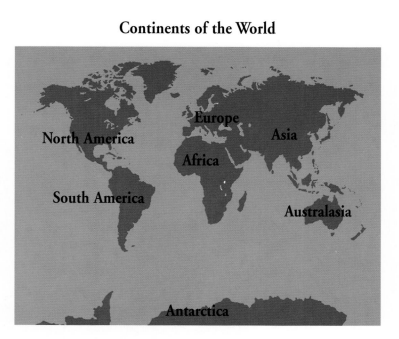

The world is divided into seven continents — North America, South America, Europe, Africa, Asia, Australasia, and Antarctica. In this book, the area where each animal lives is shown in red or blue, while all land is shown in green.

Words that appear in the glossary are printed in **boldface** type the first time they occur in the text.

American Alligator

The alligator's **snout** is wider and more rounded than a crocodile's.

The alligator's eyes and nostrils are set high on its head. This allows it to breathe and see while keeping its body hidden under water.

Its powerful jaws can grip and hold large **mammals** such as a deer or a horse.

The alligator's body is covered in hard scales to protect it from attack.

4

Alligators are large animals up to 12 feet (3.6 meters) long. They can run as fast as 35 miles per hour (56 kilometers per hour) over short distances. They **ambush** their **prey** near the water's edge.

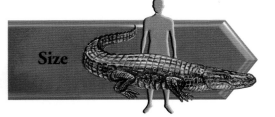
Size

2 A huge American alligator is hiding in the reeds. Only its eyes and nostrils are visible above the water. It shoots out of the river and grabs the dog in its jaws.

1 A man walks down a riverbank with his dog. The dog happily runs by the water's edge, sniffing in a clump of reeds.

3 The man cannot stop the alligator from pulling the dog out into the river. The alligator will quickly kill and eat the dog.

Where in the World

American alligators are found in the southeastern United States, mainly in the states of South Carolina, Florida, Alabama, Mississippi, Louisiana, and Texas. Most alligators now live in protected areas.

5

Marine Iguana

The marine iguana (ih-GWAH-nuh) has a spiky **crest** running along its back and tail.

The iguana's skin is very tough to stop it from injuring itself against sharp rocks.

The iguana can blow out sea salt from its nose using the fluid from special **glands**.

The iguana's feet have long claws to help it grip on to slippery rocks.

The marine iguana lives a tough life on the Galapagos Islands. It is battered by waves and scorched by the **tropical** sun. It feeds mainly on seaweed and small marine animals.

1 A marine iguana searches for seaweed along the shoreline. Small iguanas only feed on the land because their smaller bodies would get too cold if they dived into the water.

Size

2 A large marine iguana dives into the sea. It is an expert swimmer and can stay underwater for more than half an hour.

3 Diving down to depths of up to 50 feet (15 m), a marine iguana can find plenty of good seaweed on the seabed.

Green Tree Python

The green tree python can stretch its body across wide gaps between trees and branches.

The python has heat pits in front of its eyes. These pits sense the body heat of the snake's prey. The snake does not have to actually see its prey.

The snake's **pupils** are narrow during daylight to keep out the bright sunlight. They open up at night so the snake can see better in the dark.

Most of the time, the green tree python lives in the trees. Its bright green coloring allows it to hide among the leaves.

A green tree python moves easily through the jungle trees looking for prey. It can hang motionless from branches for hours, looking like a vine and waiting for victims.

1 A green tree python slithers silently into a group of trees used by roosting bats. It uses its strong tail to grip the branches. A bat suddenly flies in and lands near the snake.

2 The python raises its head slowly until it is right below the bat. It then strikes at lightning speed, grabbing the bat in its jaws and biting it with its long fangs. The python also likes to eat frogs, lizards, birds, and small mammals.

Green tree pythons were once hunted for their skin and flesh. Now, all python **species** are protected by CITES. Throughout the world, special government permission is needed to buy and sell pythons.

Where in the World

Green tree pythons live in the **rain forests** of New Guinea. It can also be found on the Cape York peninsula in northern Australia.

Emerald Tree Boa

The emerald tree boa has heat **sensors** between the scales on its lips. It uses these at night to detect the body warmth of prey.

The boa's skin is bright green to match leaves. White flecks on its skin look like patches of sunlight.

The boa's teeth are sharp and long. The snake uses them to grip and hold its prey.

The boa wraps its **prehensile** tail around branches to support it above the forest floor.

10

The emerald tree boa seems to move very slowly as it slithers along branches and through the forest. It can, however, move very fast when it is hunting and can even snatch birds in flight.

Size

1 A boa is wrapped along a jungle branch. It hangs its head low as a macaw bird flies through the air toward it.

2 As the bird flies past, the boa shoots out its head and grabs the macaw with its sharp teeth.

3 The boa wraps its coils around the macaw, squeezing it tight until it can no longer breathe. Once the bird is dead, the snake swallows the macaw head first.

Where in the World

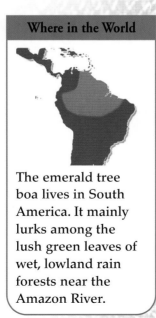

The emerald tree boa lives in South America. It mainly lurks among the lush green leaves of wet, lowland rain forests near the Amazon River.

11

Nile Crocodile

The Nile crocodile has a thick hide. **Poachers** kill the crocodile for this skin.

The crocodile uses its tail like an oar to power itself through the water.

Special clear eyelids cover the crocodile's eyes when it is swimming.

The Nile crocodile has up to sixty-eight teeth set in powerful jaws.

The Nile crocodile can grow up to 20 feet (6 m) long. Its huge size means it can eat prey as large as a fully grown wildebeest. Every year, the wildebeest **migrate** over the grassland and have to cross dangerous rivers.

Size

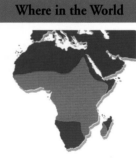

1 A wildebeest approaches a river for a drink. A crocodile is just feet away. Only its eyes poke above the water's surface. When the wildebeest gets close enough, the crocodile leaps from the water and grabs it.

2 The crocodile then drags its prey underwater, where it drowns. Afterward, the crocodile stores the **carcass** at the bottom of the river, saving it to eat later.

Did You Know?

Between 1950 and 1980, three million Nile crocodiles were killed for their skins. CITES placed the crocodile on the endangered list in the 1970s. Although it remains a protected species, it is no longer endangered.

Where in the World

Nile crocodiles are found throughout Africa. They live inside and near rivers, cooling down in the water and getting warm by **basking** on the bank.

Saltwater Crocodile

The crocodile's tail is very powerful. It is used for swimming and sometimes as a weapon.

The crocodile uses its clawed front feet to dig a nest for its eggs. The rear feet are webbed for swimming.

A saltwater crocodile grows new teeth throughout its life to replace worn teeth.

The tongue has special glands used to get rid of excess salt. These glands help the crocodile live in seawater, which is salty, as well as freshwater.

Every year, saltwater crocodiles kill hundreds of people. The crocodiles can grow up to 23 feet (7 m) long. They can kill and eat a fully grown buffalo.

1 In Malaysia, a water buffalo walks down to a river to take a drink. The saltwater crocodile glides silently up to the creature. Suddenly, it leaps from the water and grabs the buffalo by the neck.

2 The buffalo cannot struggle free. The crocodile drags it out into deep water and drowns it.

3 The crocodile shakes the carcass around violently and twists while biting, breaking the body up into bite-size pieces for eating.

Size

Where in the World

The saltwater crocodile lives in Southeast Asia and the tropical Pacific Ocean. It lives in rivers and **estuaries** and comes onto land to bask on hot days.

Rainbow Boa

The rainbow boa has bright skin colors. It mainly hunts at night when it cannot be seen.

The boa uses its muscular body to squeeze its prey to death. Its prehensile tail grips onto branches.

The snake uses its forked tongue to "taste" the air and detect prey and other boas.

The rainbow boa has heat sensors around its lips. These glands pick up the body temperature of nearby prey.

The rainbow boa likes to hunt at night. It moves silently through the trees but often likes to hunt animals that have ventured down onto the forest floor.

Size

Did You Know?

Rainbow boas are easily spotted by human hunters, who have killed them in large numbers. Also, human activity is destroying its **habitat**. Boa constrictors are on the CITES list of endangered species.

Where in the World

The rainbow boa can be found throughout the jungles of Central and South America. It divides its time between living in the trees and living on the ground.

1 A squirrel monkey drops down onto the forest floor to look for food. Above it, coiled around a branch, is a rainbow boa. Its head is hanging down as it prepares to strike. At the right moment, it springs forward and clamps its jaws around the monkey.

2 The rainbow boa wraps its coils around the monkey. It tightens them until the monkey is no longer able to breathe and dies. Then, the boa swallows its prey whole.

Gharial

The gharial (GER-ee-ul) has a long, thin snout with a large growth on the very end. The growth helps the gharial make loud noises to attract females during the **mating season**.

Grey and olive skin makes the gharial hard to spot in muddy tropical waters.

The gharial is a superb swimmer. Its long tail propels it through the water.

The gharial's feet are weak. It spends most of its time swimming; the water supports much of its weight.

Gharials' sharp, jagged teeth are ideal for catching and eating fish. Using its webbed feet and powerful tail, the gharial can move very fast through water.

1 A boy catches a large catfish on the end of his fishing line. He starts to bring it in to shore when a gharial suddenly leaps from the water with the catfish held in its mouth.

2 The fishing line snaps, and the gharial swims quickly away with its catch. It thrashes the prey from side to side to break it up into chunks for eating. The boy rushes off, scared but unharmed.

Size

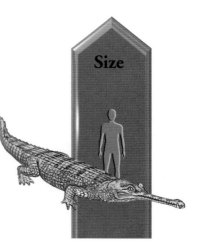

Where in the World

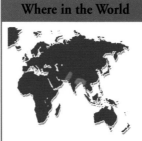

Gharials are found in rivers in northern India, Pakistan, Nepal, Bangladesh, Bhutan, and Myanmar. Wild gharials are, however, rare, and many are kept in zoos for safe breeding.

Alligator Snapping Turtle

The turtle's beak is a powerful weapon. The turtle can stab prey with it like a spear.

It uses its claws to slash prey into small pieces for eating.

The snapping turtle has a piece of wormlike flesh on its tongue, used to tempt fish into its mouth.

The turtle's strong jaws have sharp edges. These jaws cut up prey with a bone-crushing bite.

The alligator snapping turtle hunts both by day and by night. It catches its prey in jaws that are so strong they could bite through a broomstick. During the daytime, it has a sly way of luring prey to their death.

Size

Did You Know?

Humans have hunted the alligator snapping turtle for its meat. **Pesticides** from fields have also killed huge numbers by damaging its habitat. The IUCN currently lists the alligator snapping turtle as "Highly Vulnerable."

2 The fish swims into the turtle's mouth to take the "worm." At that moment, the turtle's jaws snap shut. The snapping turtle gulps down the fish in a couple of mouthfuls.

1 A snapping turtle hides in some reeds. It opens its huge mouth wide to show the wiggling pink "worm" on the end of its tongue. A fish swimming nearby sees the worm and thinks it will make an easy meal.

Where in the World

The alligator snapping turtle lives in the southeastern United States. It especially likes deep rivers, swamps, lakes, and **bayous** — anywhere it can find plenty of food.

Asian Python

The python's skin is colored like earth and plants, so it can **camouflage** itself.

Asian pythons usually have poor eyesight. They rely on smell and taste to find their way around.

The python has heat-sensitive pits inside its upper lip. It uses these to find warm-bodied prey in the dark.

The python's body is thick and muscular. Its rib cage can open up so it can swallow animals whole.

It is very rare for an Asian python to attack people, but it has happened. Pythons kill their prey using a method called "constriction." They coil around their prey and squeeze it to death.

1 An Asian python, coiled up in a tree, sees a woman approaching. Pythons often ambush their prey.

2 The python attacks by sliding quickly out of the tree and wrapping its powerful body around its prey. It tightens its coils until the victim dies, no longer able to breathe.

3 Pythons slowly eat their prey whole, opening their jaws to fit around almost any size of animal.

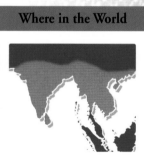

The Asian python lives in South and Southeast Asia. It inhabits areas covered by long grass, forest, and jungle. It also likes swamps.

Massasauga Rattlesnake

The massasauga (ma-suh-SAW-guh) snake shakes its tail rattle to warn enemies to keep away.

Under the bright desert sun, its pupils become thin slits to keep the extreme light out.

The massasauga's forked tongue gathers scent and passes it to its **Jacobson's organs**. These **analyze** scent, helping the snake to track down prey.

Massasaugas have a deadly **venom**. Thankfully, if they bite a human being, they rarely inject enough to kill. The experience would be terrifying and painful, however.

1 A man rides his horse along a dry riverbed in the Midwest. Ahead of him is a massasauga warming itself on some desert rocks. The snake's camouflage makes it hard to see.

Size

2 The horse steps on the massasauga's tail. The snake springs forward immediately and buries its fangs in the horse's leg. The horse rears up, attempting to shake the snake off its leg. The rider is thrown to the ground.

Where in the World

Massasaugas are found in a strip of territory reaching down from Canada to Mexico. They like to live in swamps or wild prairies. There are three types of massasauga — eastern, western, and desert varieties.

Tuatara

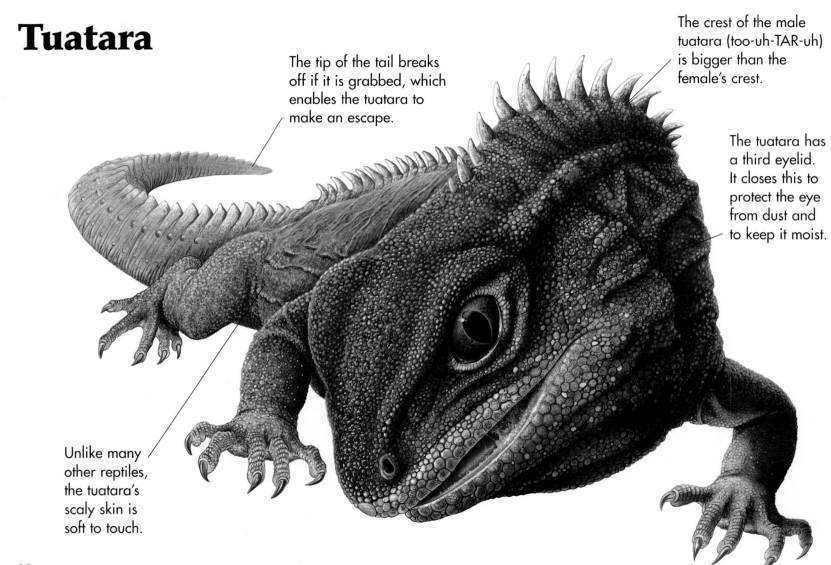

The tip of the tail breaks off if it is grabbed, which enables the tuatara to make an escape.

The crest of the male tuatara (too-uh-TAR-uh) is bigger than the female's crest.

The tuatara has a third eyelid. It closes this to protect the eye from dust and to keep it moist.

Unlike many other reptiles, the tuatara's scaly skin is soft to touch.

When tuataras were first discovered, people thought that they were lizards. Then, in 1867 a scientist named Albert Günther discovered that they were not lizards at all. Instead, they are a prehistoric type of animal more than 200 million years old.

Size

1 Tuatara skull
Günther found that tuataras have **serrated** jaw bones rather than teeth. Also, tuataras have two openings in the back of the skull called fenestrae. Most lizards have only one.

Lizard skull 2
Like people, lizards have individual teeth growing in sockets in the jawbone.

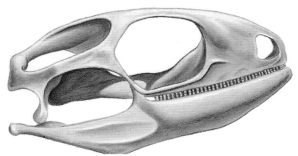

Where in the World

Tuataras used to live all over New Zealand. Their numbers fell, however, once people settled in New Zealand. Now the creatures remain only on small islands offshore. They are protected by the New Zealand government.

Komodo Dragon

The Komodo (kuh-MOE-doe) dragon is the largest lizard alive today. Males reach an average length of 10 feet (3 m) and weigh up to 300 lbs (136 kg).

Its razor-sharp teeth curve backward to grip prey. New teeth grow every three months.

The komodo dragon has a forked tongue, which can be up to 12 inches (30 centimeters) long.

It uses its knifelike claws as weapons and for digging.

The komodo dragon can kill fully grown deer, cattle, and even people with its lethal jaws. Its teeth hold lots of **bacteria**, which help kill its prey.

Size

1 A komodo dragon attacks a wild pig. It tries to knock the pig over using its tail and claws but manages only to leave deep bite marks.

2 Bacteria from the komodo dragon's teeth begin to give the pig **blood poisoning**. The dragon follows its injured prey, sometimes for days, until it finally dies.

3 The pig dies of blood poisoning. The komodo dragon quickly eats the body before finding somewhere quiet to digest the meal.

Did You Know?

There used to be hundreds of thousands of komodo dragons. Now, because of hunting and the destruction of its habitat, there are only about five thousand left. CITES lists the creature as an endangered species.

Where in the World

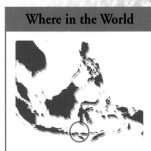

The komodo dragon is found on a remote island chain in Indonesia, with most of the animals living on Komodo Island. The islands are near the **equator** so the climate is very hot.

Glossary

ambush — to make a surprise attack from a hiding place

analyze — to make sense of something

bacteria — tiny living things that can cause infections and diseases

basking — lying in the warmth of the sun

bayous — slow-moving streams or creeks

blood poisoning — an illness caused by bacteria getting into a creature's blood

camouflage — to hide or disguise

carcass — the dead body of animal, particularly one that has been killed for food

CITES — Convention on International Trade in Endangered Species of Wild Flora and Fauna. This agreement between world governments protects endangered animals and plants from being bought and sold illegally.

crest — a ridge or plume on the head or back of an animal

endangered — to be in danger of extinction

equator — line drawn on maps to show the central point of the hot, tropical belt around the center of the world

estuaries — areas of rivers where they meet the sea and mix with saltwater

extinction — when a kind of animal or plant dies out

glands — parts of the body that make special chemicals needed by the body to work properly

habitat — a place where an animal or plant lives

IUCN — The International Union for the Conservation of Nature and Natural Resources. This organization was founded by the United Nations in 1948 to protect the natural world. It regularly draws up a "Red List" of endangered species.

Jacobson's organs — a pair of small tubes inside the throat of reptiles, used for smelling prey

mammals — animals that have a backbone, usually give birth to live young, and feed on their mother's milk

mating season — the time of year when animals make babies

migrate — to move from one place to another

pesticides — chemicals used to control plant or animal pests

poachers — people who illegally hunt and often kill animals

prehensile — able to grab or grasp

prey — animal hunted for food

pupils — the openings in the middle of the eyes through which light passes

rain forests — thick forests where a lot of rain falls

sensors — things that receive a signal and respond to it

snout — short, flat nose

serrated — jagged on the edge to cut

species — a group of living things of the same type

tropical — refering to the hottest regions of the world, with lush plant life and lots of rain

venom — a poison made by an animal

volcanic — refering to volcanoes, where hot lava pushes through the Earth, heating up the land around it

vulnerable — in danger of attack or damage